My World

Things on Wheels

by Tammy J. Schlepp

Copper Beech Books
Brookfield, Connecticut

Contents

MOVING WHEELS PAGE 4

WORKING WHEELS PAGE 14

SPECIAL WHEELS PAGE 22

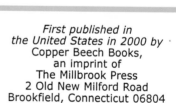

© Aladdin Books Ltd 2000

Designed and produced by
Aladdin Books Ltd
28 Percy Street
London
W1P 0LD

First published in
the United States in 2000 by
Copper Beech Books,
an imprint of
The Millbrook Press
2 Old New Milford Road
Brookfield, Connecticut 06804

Design
Flick, Book Design and Graphics

Coordinator
Jim Pipe

Picture Research
Brian Hunter Smart

Library of Congress Cataloging-in-Publication Data

Schlepp, Tammy J.
    Things on wheels / Tammy J. Schlepp.
       p. cm. -- (My world)
    Includes index.
    ISBN 0-7613-1219-6 (lib. bdg.) ; 0-7613-2336-8 (paper ed.)
       1. Motor vehicles--Wheels--Juvenile literature. 2. Vehicles--Juvenile literature. [1.
    Vehicles. 2. Motor vehicles. 3. Wheels.] I. Title. II. My world (Brookfield, Conn.)
TL270 .S36597 2000
629.2'48--dc21
                                                              00-060132

Wheels are everywhere!

See them on the street.

Spy them on the sidewalk.

They've even been to the moon!

Wheels can be big or small.

They can be used for work or play.

Bus

Buggy

What makes a wheel a wheel?

A wheel is shaped like a circle.

A wheel moves round and round.

A wheel is used for moving things.

How would you like a bicycle without wheels? It wouldn't move!

Bicycle

How does it move?

Skateboard

Look at these wheels on the skateboard and in-line skates.

What a lot of fun!

But there can be some bad falls too.

That's why it's smart
to wear a helmet
and padding.

In-line skates

Beetle

We have to push the pedals to get the wheels of a bicycle moving.

In a car or motorcycle, the engine does the work for us.

Cars are all shapes and sizes. The car above looks like a beetle.

Family car

A family car has a big trunk.

This red sports car can go fast.

Vroom! Vroom! Those wheels can move!

Sports car

School bus

Lots and lots of people need to get to lots and lots of places.

People mover

Big cars and buses get this job done, and they use big wheels to help them do it.

Train

Where is the engine?

Hundreds of people can ride on a train at one time. Trains run on tracks, not roads. Their metal wheels keep them on track.

Today there are superfast trains that whiz along at great speeds.

Big trucks may have twenty wheels or more to help them carry heavy loads.

You need special training to drive a truck this big.

Truck

The front part of the truck is called a cab.
That is where the driver sits.

The truck bends in the middle, so it can
turn in small spaces.

Fire trucks and ambulances must always be ready to go.

Fire trucks are painted a bright color so that they are easy to see.

Ambulance

The flashing lights and wailing siren mean, "Get out of the way! Someone needs help, and we must get there fast!"

Our wheels are really rolling!

Fire truck

Sometimes a motorcycle goes to the rescue!

Motorcycle

Have you seen a digger with tracks?

A track is a long belt that rolls over lots of wheels. Tracks make driving easy over bumpy ground.

Tracks

Tractor

See the ridges on these tires?
The ridges help the tractor
grip the ground.

Tires

Car tires also have ridges that
keep the car from slipping
when it turns or slows down.

Dump truck

This huge truck needs big strong
wheels to carry its heavy load.

The truck is so large, the driver has to climb up a ladder to get into the cab.

Big wheel

Some wheels have to work very hard.

Race cars wear out tires before the race is over. The crew changes all the tires in just one minute.

Racing car

Motorcycle race

Look at the wheels on these motorcycles.
They help riders lean to one side to turn
a corner.

Motorcycle racing is fast and noisy.

There are even wheels in space!

The wheels on this buggy were made to ride over the rocky ground of the moon.

Moon buggy

This space shuttle takes off like a rocket, but lands on its wheels like an airplane.

Space shuttle

Wheee! This machine on wheels
has no driver. It's a roller coaster.

It rolls up, down, and upside down.

Want a good scream?
Climb on board!

Roller coaster

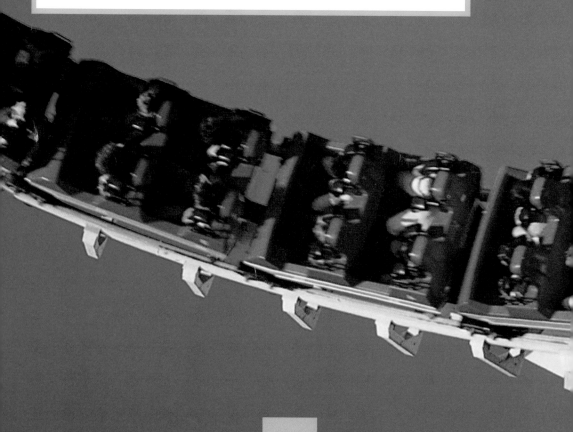

27

Can You Find?

This book is full of wheels, big and small, smooth and bumpy. Look for these wheels —where can you find them?

A

B

C

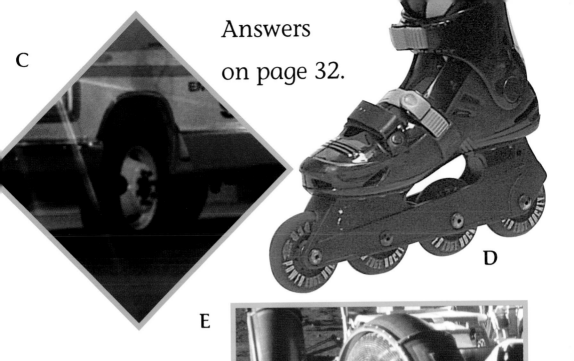

Answers on page 32.

D

E

Clue: Look at pages 5, 7, 14, 16, 19, and 24.

F

Do You Know?

People have been using wheels for thousands of years.

Do you know what these wheels are made of?

Bicycle wheels

Stagecoach wheels

30

Car wheels

Train wheel

Spacecraft
wheels

Answers on page 32.

Index

ANSWERS TO QUESTIONS

Pages 28-29 – **A** comes from a bicycle • **B** comes from a tractor • **C** comes from an ambulance • **D** comes from a pair of in-line skates • **E** comes from a moon buggy **F** comes from a truck.

Pages 30-31 – The first **bicycle wheels** were made of wood • **Stagecoach wheels** were made of wood • The first **car wheels** were made of wood • **Train wheels** are made of a metal called steel • **Spacecraft wheels** are made of light, strong metals.

Photocredits: Abbreviations: t-top, m-middle, b-bottom, r-right, l-left.
Cover, 1, 2ml, 2mr, 4, 5, 6, 12-13, 20, 21, 23, 26-27, 28l, 31mr—Digital Stock. 2tl, 7, 29tr—R. Vlitos. 2l, 3, 14-15, 29b—Scania. 8, 9 both, 11, 16-17, 22—Select Pictures. 10, 16l, 29t—Corbis. 18—John Deere. 19 both, 28r—Renault. 24, 25, 29mr—Stockbyte. 31b—NASA.
Illustrators: Peter Hutton, Alex Pang.